the
FIRST BOOK
of
WORLD
WAR
II

This book is for Harry Neil Snyder

Printed in the United States of America by the Polygraphic Company of America, Inc.

SIXTH PRINTING

Library of Congress Catalog Card Number: 58-5167

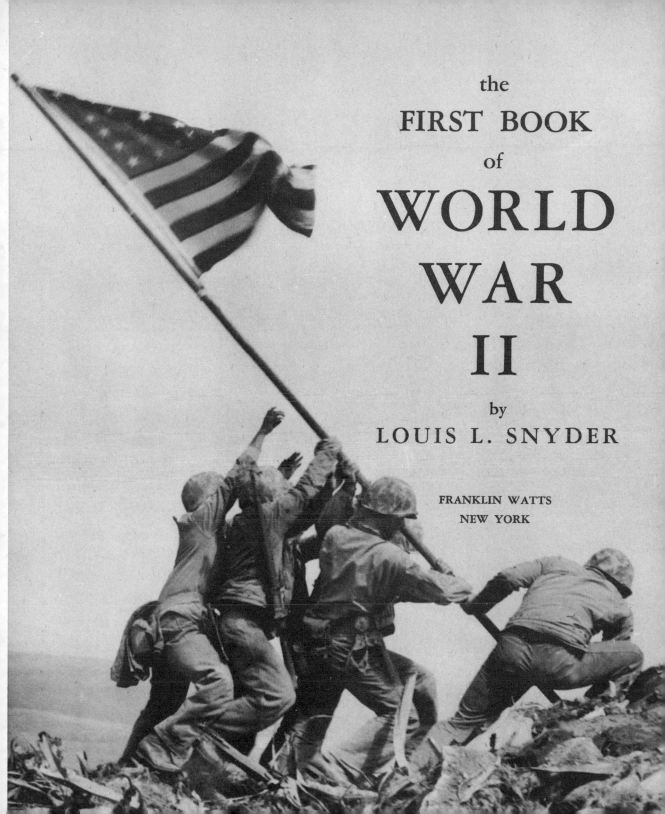

the
FIRST BOOK
of
WORLD
WAR
II

by
LOUIS L. SNYDER

FRANKLIN WATTS
NEW YORK

CONTENTS

4

THE WAR BEGINS

On September 1, 1939, the German Army crashed across the borders of Poland. First came the *Stuka* dive-bombers, with shrieking whistles in their wings, to blast the Polish planes that were on the ground. Then the German pilots bombed the railroads and highways. They smashed the big cities.

After this came the motorcycle infantry, armored cars, and tanks. Finally the regular infantry — the foot-soldiers — moved in to finish up the job.

This was a new kind of war that the Germans used. It was called *Blitzkrieg,* which is a German word meaning lightning war. The Germans had the best trained force in the world with which to wage it. The weather was good. The ground was level and just right for lightning war.

Meanwhile, the Russians were pushing into Poland from the east. They and the Germans had made a treaty to conquer and divide the country between themselves.

Poland had no chance against the mighty German army. Her little army had no time to fight back or even to begin to retreat before it was overwhelmed. Within two weeks Warsaw, the biggest city in Poland, was surrounded by the Germans. In a little over a month they had conquered the whole country and the Russians moved in from the east.

So began the six years of World War II, the most terrible war in the history of the world.

6

Nazi motorcycle infantry and armored cars enter a Polish
town after it has been devastated by repeated bombings

WHAT CAUSED WORLD WAR II

There was no one simple cause for World War II. Rather, there were many causes. Most of them grew out of World War I.

After World War I, four imperial governments were swept away — those in Germany, Austria-Hungary, Russia, and Turkey. The Germans, especially, were bitter about the terms of the Versailles Treaty which ended the war. They lost all their colonies and one-eighth of their European area. They were forced to return Alsace-Lorraine to France. Their navy, second only to Great Britain's, was almost wiped away. Their army was cut down so that it was not much larger than that of Belgium.

Late in the 18th century Poland had been divided among three countries — Russia, Prussia, and Austria, so there was no Poland when World War I ended. However, in 1919, a new independent Poland was set up in Eastern Europe. To this newly re-created country, Germany was made to give up Posen and West Prussia. This was a huge chunk of territory, 260 miles long and 80 miles wide. So that Poland could have an outlet to the sea, she was given what was called the Polish Corridor, running right through German territory. The Germans never forgave the Allies for splitting their country into two parts.

World War I was known as "the war to end wars." Instead of healing old wounds this war actually created new ones. If Germany ever got strong again, she would almost certainly try to get vengeance.

During World War I the countries allied against Germany had borrowed nearly 10 billion dollars from the United States, promising to pay it back over a period of 62 years. They expected to get the money from Germany by demanding reparations, or payments, for war damage.

Starting in 1929 there came a world-wide depression, a time when all over the world many people became poor and jobless. The depression hit Germany especially hard. She had lost almost everything she had in the war and was over her head in debt to the victorious nations.

In such times, when people are cold and hungry and see no hope ahead, it is sometimes easy for a strong and evil man to drive them where he wants them to go. Such men are called dictators. They dictate to the people, or tell them exactly what to do. They promise the people everything if only they — the dictators — are allowed to run the country. Dictators believe that human beings are like animals — strong tigers and weak lambs. They think of themselves as tigers, and believe they were born to rule the lambs.

After World War I three strong dictators arose. They were Hitler in Germany, Mussolini in Italy, and Tojo in Japan. These men called democracy a "dead corpse." In a free country they might have found it hard to make the people follow them, however fine their promises. But the Germans, the Italians, and the Japanese had never known real freedom. They were used to following strong leaders instead of working out their own problems in a democratic government.

Benito Mussolini became dictator of Italy in 1922. He was a journalist who had written a number of revolutionary pamphlets. His followers were called Fascists. When he first came into power he won the loyalty of the people by making improvements at home. He built

MUSSOLINI

TOJO

The
DICTATORS

9

HITLER

new roads, new houses, new factories. One of his proud boasts was that he had made the Italian trains run on time! But he demanded that the people obey him absolutely. Anyone who refused to obey was imprisoned or killed.

Mussolini's real ambition was to rule a great colonial empire. He told the people that Italy was overcrowded and must have more land in which to grow and become a great nation. He wanted the whole Mediterranean Sea to become an Italian lake — *Mare Nostrum,* which means Our Sea. Mussolini glorified war and conquest and sent his armies into Africa to take new land by force.

General Hideki Tojo was the leader of the war party in Japan. He won power in that tiny island by promising the people an empire in Asia. He especially wanted the Netherlands East Indies, now Indonesia, from which America got most of her tin and rubber. Under Tojo's leadership Japan attacked China in 1931. In 1932 she seized the rich province of Manchuria and renamed it Manchukuo.

Adolf Hitler became Chancellor of Germany in 1933. He was an Austrian politician who had worked his way to power through the National Socialist, or Nazi, party. His followers were called Nazis.

Hitler was a ridiculous looking little man with a screeching voice and a sick mind. But he had the power to arouse people's feelings, particularly the feeling of hate. This feeling is often strong in people suffering from hurt pride, as the Germans were after World War I. Hitler promised the half-starved Germans plenty to eat if they would do what he told them to do. He promised to win back Germany's lost territories and make her a great nation again.

Under Hitler, the Germans began to hope again. He gave them back their pride in themselves as a people. But he took away the freedom they might have found in the democratic government they had set up after World War I. No one dared go against Hitler's wishes or even disagree with him.

Hitler was driven by the idea that the German "race" was stronger and more intelligent than all others. He believed that the Germans were meant to rule mankind. He wanted to conquer Europe, and finally the whole world.

"Today, Europe," he said. "Tomorrow, the world!"

Hitler addresses members of the Hitler Youth Organization at a mass rally in Nuremberg

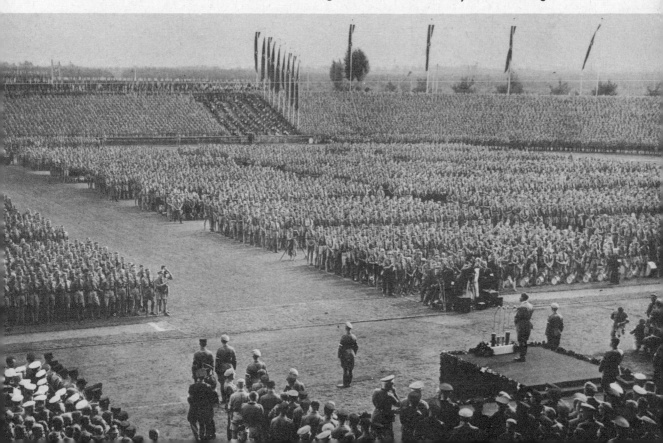

Like some German leaders before him, he worshipped war.

"For the good of the German people," he said, "we must wish for a war every fifteen or twenty years. An army whose sole purpose is to preserve peace leads only to playing at soldiers."

Once Hitler gained full power, he rounded up and imprisoned or murdered millions of Jews. He told the people that Germany's downfall was largely the fault of the Jews, and his followers believed him.

Another thing he did was to burn all the books that spoke for the freedom and dignity of the human spirit. He knew that people would be easier to lead once they got it out of their heads that they were capable of thinking for and ruling themselves.

Hitler's deeds of violence shook the world as it had not been shaken since the days of those other cruel dictators — Caligula of ancient Rome, Ivan the Terrible of Russia, and Philip II of Spain.

In 1936 Hitler and Mussolini joined forces in what was called the Rome-Berlin Axis. It was called "Axis" because all the European states were supposed to revolve around the two great powers of Germany and Italy, as a wheel revolves around its axle.

On September 27, 1940, Japan joined the Axis. Now it was called the Pact of Steel. The three dictator nations, Italy, Germany, and Japan, planned to conquer the world and divide it between them.

The German plan was to take over Europe piece by piece. The Italian plan was to cooperate with Hitler and get what was left over in Europe and as much of Africa as could be conquered. The Japanese plan was to create a huge empire in the Far East.

Mussolini stands in the saddle to address a meeting of the Fascist Youth Organization

Hitler, Mussolini, and Tojo felt strong and sure of themselves. It was impossible to reason with them. They wanted war. They started it. The Allies — Britain and France, and later Russia and the United States — tried to stop them.

The blame for *starting* World War II rests solely and squarely on the Axis powers.

13

HITLER'S CONQUEST OF EUROPE

Hitler began his conquest of Europe in 1938. On March 15 of that year he sent his troops into Austria. Nobody lifted a hand to stop him when he occupied that country and proclaimed it part of Germany.

Next Hitler decided to take over Czechoslovakia. This new democratic republic had been formed out of a part of the old Austro-Hungarian Empire after World War I. It included the region called the Sudetenland. There were a great many Germans living in this area. Hitler claimed falsely that they were mistreated. He threatened to seize the Sudetenland by force.

Both France and Russia had signed treaties to defend Czechoslovakia. If Hitler attacked her, they were bound to come to her help. If war came, Britain would surely be drawn into it. And Britain was not prepared for war.

In an effort to keep the peace, Britain's elderly Prime Minister, Neville Chamberlain, and the French Premier, Édouard Daladier, went to Germany to talk to Hitler. They met both Hitler and Mussolini at the city of Munich. There, on September 29, 1938, all four signed the document known as the Munich Pact.

By the Munich Pact war was stopped at the last minute. But it was done at a cruel price, and on Hitler's own terms. The document gave Germany 11,000 miles of Czech territory. This territory contained more than 3,000,000 people. The broken little country was left at the mercy of Hitler.

Chamberlain returned to London waving a piece of paper. He as-

Prime Minister Neville Chamberlain is greeted by crowds as he returns from his historic conference with Hitler on Czechoslovakia. Chamberlain's umbrella, which he carried rain or shine, became a symbol of "appeasement," or trying to get along with Hitler on the dictator's own terms

sured the English people that he had brought "peace in our time."

No one asked the poor Czechs how they felt about it. And the betrayal of Czechoslovakia did not bring peace. Before the year was over, England and France had reason to suspect that Germany planned to invade Poland.

After World War I France had signed a treaty with Poland promising to protect her if she were invaded. Now, as it became clear that Hitler had his eyes on Poland, England announced that she, too, would fight to protect her. This was the end of appeasement. On September 3, 1939, France and England declared war on Germany.

The AXIS in EUROPE, 1939

- The AXIS: Germany, Italy and occupied territory at the close of 1939

NORWAY SWEDEN FINLAND

DENMARK

GREAT BRITAIN

GERMANY

Warsaw POLAND

UNION OF SOVIET SOCIALIST REPUBLICS

(RUSSIA)

CZECHOSLOVAKIA

FRANCE

Munich

SWITZERLAND AUSTRIA HUNGARY

RUMANIA

YUGOSLAVIA

ITALY

BULGARIA

SPAIN

ALBANIA GREECE

TURKEY

Nazi infantry on the march in Poland

THE SINKING OF THE ATHENIA

World War II was only nine hours old on that beautiful September day. The passengers on board the *Athenia,* a Cunard liner traveling from London to Montreal, were enjoying themselves. Suddenly some one cried,

"Look! There's a torpedo!"

Almost at once there was a crashing explosion and the unarmed ship began to sink. Women and children were rushed into the life-boats. But nearly a hundred people lost their lives.

The British had not yet done anything to protect their ships at sea. The sinking of the *Athenia* gave the world warning that once again the Germans would do everything in their power to break British control of the seas, just as they had tried to do in World War I.

THE "PHONY WAR"

On land, nothing much happened for awhile after war was declared. People began to call World War II the "phony war." The Germans called it the *Sitzkrieg,* which means sit-down war.

The French dug in behind their great Maginot Line — a long series of underground forts running along the border between France and Germany. The Germans stayed behind their Siegfried Line, or West Wall, which they had hastily built above ground. Both sides could see each other. There was little shooting.

Some of the Allied soldiers sang a song — "I'll Hang Out My Washing on the Siegfried Line!"

One of the reasons for this strange lack of fighting was the fact that the winter of 1939-1940 was one of the worst in living memory. Another reason was that Hitler secretly planned to turn on his partner, Russia, in the east. He thought he could get out of fighting the French and English by defeating the Russians. Once Russia was conquered he would turn to the Allies and say,

"See, we Germans don't like the Russian Communists any more than you do. Look how strong we are! Now let us make peace."

→

An American soldier plays the bagpipes in the "Dragon's Teeth" of the Siegfried line

ADOLF HITLER, 1940: "I am convinced that our struggle will in the future be blessed by Providence as it has been blessed up to now. I look to the future with fanatical confidence."

BLITZKRIEG *IN THE WEST*

Before turning on Russia, Hitler wanted to be stronger in western Europe. Suddenly, in early April, 1940, he attacked Denmark and Norway. He took them in a single day. His *Blitzkrieg* was like a knife cutting through butter.

A month later Hitler struck again. He invaded Holland and Belgium. German tanks, followed by infantry, crashed across the borders of these two small countries. Parachutists took airfields, bridges, and railroads. The German Air Force, or *Luftwaffe,* bombed the center of Rotterdam, in Holland, leaving it in flames.

At this time Winston Churchill became Prime Minister of England. The British people hoped he would find a quick way out of the war.

"I have nothing to offer but blood, toil, tears, and sweat," he said.

20

MIRACLE AT DUNKIRK

By 1940 things looked dark for the Allies. Their combined efforts had failed to halt Hitler's advance into Belgium.

At the northeastern corner of France was stationed a British expeditionary force, together with French troops. They intended to keep the Germans from sweeping on to Paris. Then, on May 28, King Leopold of Belgium ordered his army to surrender to the Germans. This was a serious blow to the Allies. The Belgians had been guarding one flank, or side, of the Allied front. Now the Germans sent a *Panzer,* or tank column, racing westward to the English Channel.

This left the British and French troops to the north separated from the main French armies. They were caught in a trap. They pulled back to Dunkirk on the coast of France, the only seaport that the enemy had not captured. They had to leave the Continent or be wiped out.

Between the retreating Allied armies and the Germans there was a series of flood gates, used to protect Dunkirk from the waters of the North Sea. The British opened these flood gates so that the waters would flow in and hold up the Germans. Actually, it didn't help much. The Allied Army of half a million men, mostly British, with a few Dutch and the remains of the French army, were strafed or bombed continuously as they poured into the tiny city of Dunkirk. They were forced into an ever narrowing space toward the beaches, with only the sea ahead.

For a few days British and French aircraft controlled the air. They

21

were helped by the weather, which was cloudy. The rear guard fought desperately on the outskirts of Dunkirk. But the men crowding onto the beaches knew that time was running out. Many of them were wounded, sick, or dying. It seemed they would all be butchered by the Germans.

Meanwhile, a strange rescue fleet set out from England. Never before did such a fleet go to war. There were motorboats, lifeboats, French fishing boats, navy whalers, tugboats, sailboats, Channel ferries, sloops, mine-sweepers — almost anything that would float.

These boats were manned by every kind of Englishman. There were bankers and dentists, taxicab drivers and clerks, fishermen and policemen. There were old men whose skins looked fiery red against their white hair. There were bright-faced young Sea Scouts, off on the great adventure of their lives. They were all wet, chilled to the bone, hungry. They were unarmed, but they sailed bravely toward Dunkirk into waters covered with the oil of sunken ships.

Some skippers steered by the flames from Dunkirk. Others just followed in line. Some lost their lives in the darkness when destroyers cut their little crafts into two. Others were battered and broken by German fighter planes. Still the strange fleet sailed on while the British planes dropped bombs to put a wall of flame between the retreating forces and the Germans who were chasing them.

As the boats approached the beaches, men waded out by the thousands to board them. Others dropped from the ruined piers. Packed beyond the limits of safety, the boats sailed back to England, only to return for more men.

Troops being evacuated from the beaches of Dunkirk

Out of the rescue boats onto the soil of England stepped an army of dirty, sleepy, hungry men. They were so tired they could hardly walk. One reporter said that they brought with them half the dog population of Belgium and France.

"Some of the dogs were shell-shocked. They whimpered but the men didn't!"

Dunkirk was a turning point in World War II. What seemed to be a great defeat was turned into a great moral victory — a victory in which the defeated soldiers performed so splendidly that they lived to fight another day. Carried out under the eyes and fire of the enemy, the retreat saved a whole British army.

The retreat also inspired the greatest voice in England. After the miracle of Dunkirk, Churchill made this proud challenge:

"We shall fight on the seas and oceans. We shall fight with growing confidence and growing strength in the air. We shall defend our island, whatever the cost may be. We shall fight on the beaches. We shall fight on the landing grounds. We shall fight in the fields and in the streets. We shall fight in the hills. We shall never surrender!"

→

WINSTON CHURCHILL: *(after Dunkirk)* "The little ships, the unforgotten, un-Homeric catalogue of *Mary Jane* and *Peggy IV*, of *Folkstone Belle, Boy Billy,* and *Ethel Maud,* of *Lady Haig* and *Skylark* . . . the little ships of England brought the army home."

U-BOAT WAR IN THE ATLANTIC

On the Atlantic Ocean other battles were being fought. Since the British Navy was too strong for them on the surface of the seas, the Germans depended most of all on their fleet of submarines. These were called U-boats or Undersea-boats.

In World War I the Germans had sent out their U-boats singly. Now they hunted in "wolf packs," with a fleet of supply ships for refueling and minor repairs at sea. At night the U-boats traveled at full speed on the surface. During the day they would go under the surface and wait to prey on Allied shipping.

The Battle of the Atlantic was like a game of hide-and-seek, played over endless miles of ocean. Allied ships traveled together in convoys guarded by small warships called destroyers. From these sleek, fast destroyers huge "ash-cans," filled with explosives, were thrown overboard to destroy the submarines.

The battle moved over the whole of the Atlantic. As soon as the enemy found it too hot for him in one area, he went somewhere else.

These U-boats took a terrible toll of ships. They had to be beaten if the war was to be won.

The 16 inch guns of an Allied battleship release their charges in a burst of flame and smoke

Nazi troops entering Paris

FRANCE FALLS

With the British gone, the Germans overran the Continent.

The French believed that theirs was the finest army in the world. They felt safe behind their Maginot Line. But Hitler went right around the line. The huge French armies reeled back in retreat. Before long the Germans were hammering at the gates of Paris.

The roads were jammed with people trying to escape. They pushed wagons, baby carriages, anything that would move. Then the Nazi planes came swooping out of the sky and poured death and destruction on these helpless people.

Within a few weeks all of northern France was occupied by the Nazi hordes. And Mussolini, knowing that France was about to fall, declared war on France and Britain.

On June 17 a German officer hurried to a garden behind the front lines where Hitler was pacing nervously up and down.

"My Leader," said the officer, "the French have given up. Marshal Pétain has just spoken on the radio. He said, 'The continuation of the struggle against an enemy superior in numbers and in arms is futile. It is with a heavy heart I say we must cease the fight.'"

Then a curious thing happened. Hitler was so happy that he could not control the twitching in his legs. Suddenly he started to dance a jig of joy. He jumped up and down like a dancer on a stick!

The French surrendered on June 21, 1940, in a little clearing in the forest of Compiègne. This was the exact spot where the Germans had surrendered to the French after World War I.

THE BATTLE OF BRITAIN

Now Britain stood alone, and the Germans sang,

"We challenge the lion of England,
For the last and decisive cup,

We judge and we say
An Empire breaks up.
Listen to the engine singing — get on to the foe!
Listen, in your ears it's ringing — get on to the foe!

BOMBS, OH BOMBS, OH BOMBS ON ENGLAND!"

Hundreds of German *Stuka* dive-bombers, *Dorniers,* and *Heinkels* roared over the English Channel and dropped their cargoes of death. They came mostly at night. They were trying to soften up England for a German invasion. It was to be called Operation Sea-Lion.

"This wicked man Hitler," said Churchill, "has now resolved to break down our famous island race."

London was heavily hit. Bombs fell on the slums. Even Buckingham Palace was hit. Londoners will never forget the night the German bombs started 1,500 separate fires in the heart of the city. Old and famous buildings were wrecked.

But Adolf Hitler did not know the courage and strength of the people he was trying to beat down. The British people remained firm

29

A German officer snapped
this picture of Hitler doing his
"victory jig"

and calm while night after sleepless night the bombs fell on their cities. There was no panic. From king to clerk to office boy they showed an astonishing spirit. The two young princesses, Elizabeth and Margaret Rose, stayed in England during the heavy air attacks.

The British worked out a good defense against the air raids. By radar, an electronic beam that bounces off objects in space, they could detect enemy planes far away. "Spotters" watched the skies night and day. Anti-aircraft guns ringed the cities. The British even hung piano wire from balloons, and some Nazi planes were caught in it. Thousands of men, women, boys, and girls acted as fire-watchers.

But most important of all was the Royal Air Force — the R.A.F. It was made up of just a few hundred young fighter-pilots. Some were not yet twenty years old. In speedy *Hurricanes* and *Spitfires* they rose to challenge the Germans.

St. Paul's Cathedral surrounded by smoke and flame during an air raid on London

30

A gunner of the London Home Guard camouflaged by blackened face and old wall paper is ready to take up his post in a bombed-out house if the Germans invade England

In three months these young pilots destroyed more than 2,000 Nazi planes. The Germans were forced to give up their plan for the immediate invasion of Britain.

The Battle of Britain was the first air war in history. It was also the first German defeat of World War II. The British people knew what they owed to the tireless young pilots of the R.A.F. In a speech before the House of Commons, Winston Churchill said,

"Never in the field of human conflict was so much owed by so many to so few."

A German armored car crosses a temporary bridge built to replace one destroyed by Greek patriots

THE BATTLE OF THE BALKANS

In the years following the fall of France, the Axis forces overran the Balkan countries in southeastern Europe. This gave them a great advantage over the Allies, for the area is a kind of land bridge to Asia.

Hungary was already under German influence. By October, 1940, Hitler had occupied Rumania with its great Ploesti oil fields. Rumania joined the Axis powers on March 1, 1941.

But Greece fought back bravely. Her army hurled back the Italians when they tried to invade her through Albania. Mussolini begged Germany for help, and it came in the usual *Blitzkrieg* fashion. By May 20, 1941, the Germans held all of Greece.

These conquests not only gave the Germans control of the Balkans, but also made them a serious threat in the Mediterranean Sea. The water route to India, by way of Gibraltar, Suez, and Aden, was now endangered. This route was called Britain's "life line." It was necessary to her for moving supplies to her armies in the East.

33

During the four years they were besieged by bombs and long-range guns the people of Dover, England, lived in caves hollowed out of the chalk cliffs

THE TRAITORS

In smashing his way to control of the Continent, Hitler had the help of men who betrayed their own countries. These traitors were known as "collaborationists." They collaborated with, or helped, the Nazis as they stormed into the various countries. One of the most infamous of the collaborationists was Vidkun Quisling of Norway. His name has come to mean a person who is a self-seeking traitor. Quisling ruled Norway for five years in the full glory of Hitler's approval, only to be shot by a Norwegian firing squad when the Nazi government crumbled.

In France Henri Pétain, hero of World War I, helped the Germans. So did the statesman Pierre Laval. Each occupied country had its share of these collaborationists.

A *Goumier*, or French colonial soldier from Morocco

THE WAR BEHIND THE LINES

Millions of people were forced into the Nazi "new order." There were Poles, Czechs, Danes, Norwegians, Netherlanders, Belgians, French, Jugoslavs, and Greeks. Many of them had to work as slave laborers in Nazi factories.

But inside their own countries the peoples of Europe refused to stay beaten. They carried on a war behind the lines.

The Czechs wrecked trucks and blew up ammunition dumps. In the factories they put powdered glass into oil and sugar into gasoline to spoil them. They made bullets and shells which would not explode.

Hollanders killed Nazi officers and soldiers. In the middle of the night they would put iron weights on the bodies and throw them into the canals, where they would not be found.

Norwegians wrecked telephone, telegraph, and electric lines. They started fires and explosions.

The French resisted by blowing up bridges and derailing trains.

← The Free French, under General Charles de Gaulle, fought the Axis after France fell. Here Free French sailors check the engine room of the submarine *Rubis*, about to leave on patrol duty

They published patriotic newspapers right under the noses of the enemy.

And everywhere throughout Europe there were brave people who helped captured Allied prisoners to escape.

The peoples of Europe became united in their hate for the invaders.

The German occupation forces reacted violently. If one of their men were killed, they took hostages, or prisoners. They would arrest anybody in sight, including children, and put them to death in revenge. They warned, "Fifty Frenchmen for every German killed!"

Hundreds of innocent men, women, and children were executed.

One of Hitler's most savage lieutenants was Reinhard Heydrich, "the Savage Hangman." Czech patriots killed him, and the Nazis took terrible revenge. In the little Czechoslovakian village of Lidice, where one of the slayers was believed to be hiding, the Nazis did a senseless, brutal thing. They lined up every man, 190 in all, on a grassy meadow and machine-gunned them. The 195 women in town were sent to a concentration camp. And the 82 children were scattered abroad. Then every trace of Lidice was destroyed, even its graveyard, and the ground was plowed flat.

"The name Lidice has been wiped from the face of the earth forever!" shouted the Nazi radio.

But the Nazi radio was wrong. Today, at the spot where the little village stood, thousands of visitors pass by to see the monument that has made Lidice immortal.

The German policy of terror did not work. For terror breeds terror. And the world does not forget.

HITLER, MASTER OF EUROPE

By the Spring of 1941 Hitler was the master of all Europe. He seemed unbeatable. Germany had increased her size from 180,976 to 323,360 square miles, plus 290,000 more in lands which she had occupied but not made part of her Empire. Her population had jumped from 65,000,000 to 106,000,000. Hitler had 40,000 airplanes, 180 submarines, 363,171 tons of surface navy, 214 infantry divisions, and 12 *Panzer* divisions. Against this powerful force was pitted the might of the British Commonwealth, and a worldwide opinion opposed to Nazi aggression. There was also something else Hitler had not counted on — the resources of the United States.

HITLER'S EUROPE, 1941

The AXIS and occupied territory

The greatest extent of Hitler's invasion of Russia

NORWAY
SWEDEN
FINLAND
Leningrad
Moscow
UNION OF SOVIET SOCIALIST REPUBLICS (RUSSIA)
DENMARK
GREAT BRITAIN
London
HOLLAND
GERMANY
Rotterdam
POLAND
Dunkirk
Stalingrad
BELGIUM
Lidice
Calais
Compiègne
CZECHOSLOVAKIA
Paris
SWITZERLAND
AUSTRIA
HUNGARY
FRANCE
RUMANIA
Yalta
YUGOSLAVIA
Ploesti
PORTUGAL
ITALY
BULGARIA
SPAIN
ALBANIA
GREECE
TURKEY

THE ARSENAL OF DEMOCRACY

The United States had hoped to stay out of the war. But as the struggle went on she began to realize that she would have to join the fight in some way. The growing power of Hitler threatened not only the rights of Europeans but of Americans also. The United States was the only nation which could outmatch the industrial might of Hitler's Europe. Without her help it was doubtful if Britain could have continued the war after the fall of France.

After only a year of struggle the British had spent most of their money buying food and war materials from the United States. Their plight was solved on March 11, 1941, when the United States passed the Lend-Lease Bill. Under this act, "any country whose defense the President deemed vital for the defense of the United States" might receive war goods from the United States by sale, exchange, or loan.

The United States told the world her plans by means of the Atlantic Charter. In August, 1941, President Franklin D. Roosevelt and Prime Minister Winston Churchill met off the coast of Newfoundland to draw up this document. In it they pledged allegiance to democracy and promised to work for a world in which all nations would be equal "after the final destruction of the Nazi tyranny."

The United States now became the arsenal, or storehouse, of democracy. From her farms poured the food, from her factories the weapons that would overthrow the dictators.

→

When the Germans neared Leningrad, old men, women, and children went out to build a girdle of fortifications around the city

HITLER TURNS ON RUSSIA

Suddenly, on Sunday morning, June 22, 1941, Germany turned on her ally, Russia. On this same day, back in 1812, the French conqueror Napoleon Bonaparte had attacked Russia. Hitler, who fancied himself a second Napoleon, thought it was his lucky day.

Three huge German armies crossed the Russian border without meeting any great resistance. They headed for Leningrad in the north, Moscow in the center, and Stalingrad in the South.

"Russia is broken!" shouted Hitler. "She will never rise again!"

At first many of the Russian people welcomed Hitler because they thought he had come to free them from their own dictator, Joseph Stalin. But Hitler proved to be even worse, they felt, than Stalin. He put many Russians to death and treated the rest as slaves. The Russian people rose to defend their homeland.

The Russians astonished the whole world by their fierce resistance. It wasn't only the soldiers who fought, but the old men, the women, the children as well. They burned their own homes and factories. They blew up bridges. They dynamited their huge dams. They destroyed everything in the path of the Germans.

When they were hopelessly surrounded, the Russians fought even harder. Like the early American Indians, they disappeared into the forests, coming out only at night to smash the railroads or kill the German guards.

Help came at last from Britain and America in the form of war materials.

Hitler was so sure of his own strength that he believed Russia would fall in six weeks. He was wrong. He did not reckon with the Russian climate, especially the severe winters. His soldiers did not even have winter clothing. And the Russian winter of 1941 turned out to be the worst anyone could remember.

Caught in the icy mud, the huge German war machine slowed down to a crawl on the Russian plains. Hitler, who boasted that he never was wrong, had to explain to his people. He said,

"We made a mistake about one thing. We did not know how strong the Russians were."

Russian children attend classes on the steps of their bombed-out school

On August 22, 1942, the Germans began their first direct attack on Stalingrad. For three months a savage battle raged for this Russian city. So closely were the opposing forces matched that the capture of two or three yards, or even one building, was big news. Shells churned the rubble day after day. A huge German army outside the city struck again and again. But Stalingrad held out.

Soon the Germans were in full flight along a front of many hundreds of miles. The retreat was just like that of Napoleon's army in 1812. The plains of Russia were filled with smashed and burned war machines, wrecked vehicles, and the twisted figures of the dead.

Stalingrad was disaster for Nazi Germany.

"A DATE WHICH WILL LIVE IN INFAMY"

While the United States watched the struggle in Europe, her relations with Japan grew steadily worse. She resented the growth of Japanese sea and air power in the Pacific area. If Japan became master of eastern Asia she would interfere with United States trade and business interests there. Japan's brutalities in China, her joining of the Axis in 1940, had made it clear that Japan was embarked upon as ruthless a conquest of the free world as Germany was.

For their part, the Japanese were bitter because of what they called America's interference in their plan to create an Empire in eastern Asia. They felt that she stood in their way to further conquests. Still, they dared not risk an open break with her until Hitler's first successes in Russia made it seem likely that the Axis would win the war. Like the Italian Fascists, the followers of Tojo were willing to risk their necks only on the winning side!

At 7:55 on the morning of December 7, 1941, a messenger boy pedaled his bicycle in the direction of the American naval station at Pearl Harbor, in Hawaii. He carried a telegram from General George C. Marshall, the Chief of Staff in Washington, to the commanding officer at Pearl Harbor. The telegram warned the naval station to be on the alert for a Japanese attack.

Suddenly there was a tremendous explosion.

"Wow!" said the messenger boy, " that's not a joke!"

He dived into a ditch. And he had to stay there for the next few hours while bombs fell all around him.

There had been signs earlier that something was wrong. At 6:45 that morning a patrolling American destroyer, the *Ward,* had found and sunk a Japanese midget submarine in waters where no Japanese submarine had the right to be. Two army privates, working at a radar station, spotted planes many miles away. They were worried, but their lieutenant said that the planes were probably American B-17's.

It was Sunday morning and most of the ship and plane crews were on holiday leave.

Then it happened. Flying low out of the morning haze came the first wave of Japanese bombers. The round red emblem of Japan shone on their wings. The bombs began to drop.

It was a murderous attack. The battleship *Arizona* was almost completely destroyed by a direct hit. The *Oklahoma,* struck by many

Wrecked foremast of the *U.S.S. Arizona* after the attack on Pearl Harbor

43

A small boat rescues a seaman from the water near the blazing U.S.S. *West Virginia* during the attack on Pearl Harbor

torpedoes, turned over and sank in shallow water. In all, some fourteen big warships and many smaller ships were wrecked or damaged. United States planes were smashed to bits on the ground before ever they had a chance to rise. In a matter of minutes American naval and air power in the Hawaiian Islands was paralyzed. Nearly 2,500 soldiers, sailors, and civilians died in the blazing inferno, most of them Americans.

In Washington, Secretary of State Cordell Hull got news of the disaster quickly. Before he had gotten over the shock of it, an aide came into his office and told him that two Japanese envoys were waiting outside to see him.

"What do they want?" the Secretary asked.

"They have a note for you, sir."

"While bombs are falling on Pearl Harbor! Tell them to wait."

Mr. Hull let the two Japanese cool their heels a while in the outer office before he let them in. He read the note, which was filled with insults. Then he let the envoys have it!

Mr. Hull had been born and raised in the hills of Tennessee. He knew some colorful curse words, and he is said to have used them freely on the Japanese envoys. Usually a man in his position would not speak this way. But, like all Americans, he was boiling. Finally, in a voice choked with emotion, he said,

"I must say that in fifty years of public service I have never seen a note that was crowded with such lies. I never imagined until today that any government in this world was capable of uttering them."

Then he coldly told the two Japanese to leave his office.

In Japan Emperor Hirohito announced to the people,

"We, by the grace of Heaven, Emperor of Japan, seated on the throne of a line for ages eternal, say to you, our loyal and brave subjects: We hereby declare war on the United States of America and the British Empire."

The next day, in America, President Franklin D. Roosevelt read a message to Congress. It opened with the words,

"Yesterday, December 7, 1941 . . . a date which will live in infamy . . ."

With only a single "no" vote, Congress declared war on Japan.

Speaking for a nation united, President Roosevelt said:

"We are now in this war. We are in it all the way. Every single man, woman, and child is a partner in the most tremendous undertaking in our national history."

Three days later, on December 10, 1941, carrying out their "Pact of Steel," Germany and Italy declared war on the United States.

Thus, by declaring war on Japan, America found herself with *two* wars on her hands.

→

FRANKLIN DELANO ROOSEVELT: *(speech to the nation after Pearl Harbor)* "We are now in the midst of a war, not for conquest, not for vengeance, but for a world in which this nation, and all that this nation represents, will be safe for our children"

THE JAPANESE IN THE PACIFIC

Soon after Pearl Harbor Japan began to spread all over the Pacific. In four days she attacked Singapore, Manila, Wake, and Guam. She landed troops all over the Far East.

Japanese planes sank the huge British battleship *Prince of Wales* and the battle-cruiser *Repulse*. A weary British garrison surrendered in Singapore. The Japanese also captured the important Burma Road, the supply route to China from India.

In the Philippines the outnumbered, starving Americans fought heroically, but in vain. General Douglas MacArthur, on orders from President Roosevelt, escaped from Bataan to Australia.

"I shall return!" said General MacArthur.

The Americans made a last stand at Bataan. Under command of Lieutenant General Jonathan Wainwright, the gallant Filipino-American defenders were bombarded from the air, pounded with heavy artillery, and attacked by infantry units. At last they surrendered. The Japanese captured 11,500 prisoners. These unfortunate men, with their commander General Wainwright, were taken by the Japanese on a horrible death march. Sick, starved, and miserable, prodded by Japanese bayonets, they were forced to walk for scores of miles to a prisoners' camp. Hundreds perished on the way.

Bataan became a household word in the United States. Americans would remember "Bataan" just as they would remember Pearl Harbor.

Soon the Japanese overran the Netherlands East Indies. The Rising Sun of Japan was now dangerously close to Australia and India.

48

Dead American soldiers on a beach in New Guinea

THE HOME FRONT

In a great war there are two fronts — the battle front where the soldiers fight, and the home front where the people work to support their fighting men.

Within a year after Pearl Harbor millions of Americans went into factories and shipyards to work. They promised not to go on strike as long as the war lasted. Americans started a shipbuilding program that fulfilled the slogan "A ship a day!" And out of their factories poured planes, landing craft, tanks, trucks, and rifles — all the tools of war.

Boys and girls did their share, too. They went searching in attics, basements, yards, and vacant lots for scrap metal. They found old iron, tin, brass, copper, tinfoil, all kinds of metal that could be melted down and used again. They also sold war bonds to help raise money for the war. Millions of boys and girls were heroes on the home front and helped to win the biggest war in history.

THE WAR IN NORTH AFRICA

Once Hitler had conquered Europe, he could be attacked only from Britain, from Russia, or from North Africa. North Africa thus became one of the most important battle fronts of World War II.

When the war began, Mussolini had sent his troops to North Africa. His strategy was to capture the Suez Canal and thus cut off the Allies from the Far East. The British had troops in Egypt, some stationed there before the war and others brought there all the way round Africa. They planned to capture all of North Africa, and then use it as a base for an attack on Hitler's Fortress Europe.

By 1941 Italian troops had already driven 60 miles into Egypt toward the Suez Canal. Then British forces struck back. Their surprise attack carried them eastward halfway across Libya. They captured many Italian prisoners.

Again Mussolini called on Hitler for help. Together, the Germans and Italians drove the British back into Egypt.

The first round of the Battle of North Africa ended in a draw.

Round two came in 1942. Once again it was a seesaw battle swinging back and forth. Desert warfare was a story of fast-moving tanks pushing forward through the enemy lines and then retreating across the hot sands.

General Erwin Rommel was the German leader. He was a brilliant master of tank warfare. He was called the Desert Fox because he was as wily and shrewd as a fox. He led his tanks into Egypt.

It was a dark moment for the British. But their Eighth Army, under

← Women putting the finishing touches on inflatable life rafts for the U. S. Navy

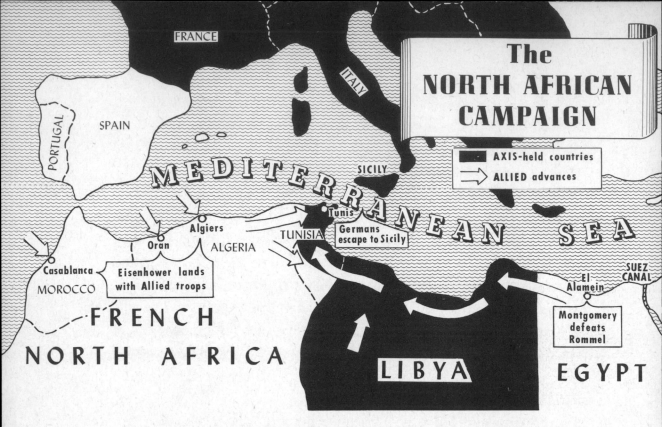

The NORTH AFRICAN CAMPAIGN

AXIS-held countries
ALLIED advances

FRANCE
PORTUGAL
SPAIN
MEDITERRANEAN SEA
SICILY
ITALY
Tunis
TUNISIA
Germans escape to Sicily
Algiers
Oran
ALGERIA
Casablanca
MOROCCO
Eisenhower lands with Allied troops
FRENCH NORTH AFRICA
LIBYA
EGYPT
El Alamein
SUEZ CANAL
Montgomery defeats Rommel

the command of General Bernard Montgomery, beat the Germans at El Alamein. It was one of the greatest victories of the war.

While Montgomery was chasing the Desert Fox, there came a sensational surprise far to the west. In French North Africa, three Anglo-American landings were made at Casablanca, Oran, and Algiers. Troops, tanks, and tons of supplies were put ashore safely from a vast fleet of ships. It was a magnificent feat. It came as a complete surprise to the Axis war leaders.

The commander of this expedition was the great General Dwight D. Eisenhower.

The enemy was now caught in a pincers movement from both east and west. Hitler poured thousands of air-borne troops into the battle. But it was all in vain.

Round three came in 1943.

Montgomery pursued the Desert Fox westward for more than a thousand miles. British tanks moved as much as forty miles a day. And Eisenhower closed in from the west. The Germans were caught in a steel trap.

The Germans, with their usual skill, fought hard. But the end, when it came, came quickly. Cut off by land, sea, and air, without any oil for their tanks, they were helpless.

What was left of Hitler's African army escaped to Europe. They

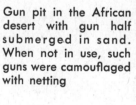

Gun pit in the African desert with gun half submerged in sand. When not in use, such guns were camouflaged with netting

Allied troops advance over hilly country in North Africa

crossed the narrow straits between Tunis and Sicily, the island off the toe of Italy. The Italians lost their African armies and all their African possessions.

Now the way was open to attack Hitler from the south, "the soft under-belly of the Axis," as Churchill called it, where the defenses were not as strong as in the north.

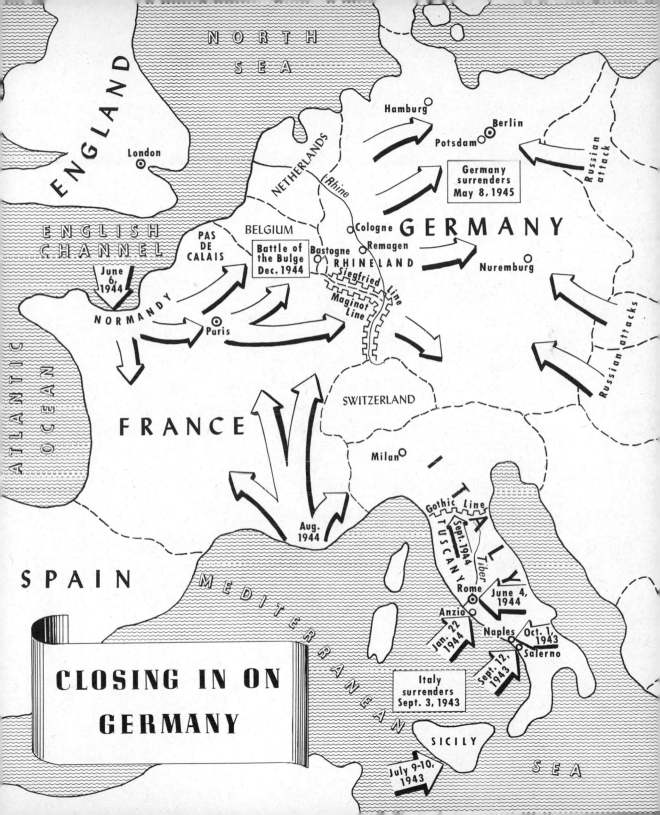

THE BEGINNING OF THE END

Now that Mussolini's dreams of empire in North Africa had been blasted, the Allies planned to invade Italy and advance straight up the peninsula toward Germany.

Over July 9 and 10, 1943, the Allied armies crossed from North Africa to Sicily. The Italians surrendered in droves. By August 17 the conquest of Sicily was complete. President Roosevelt announced that "it was the beginning of the end" for the dictators.

When the Italian people saw Sicily and their colonies conquered, their armies destroyed, and their cities ruined, they threw out their dictator, Mussolini, with his fake promises. And on September 3, 1943, the Italian government surrendered to the Allies.

The Allied armies stationed in Sicily now crossed over to Italy itself. They landed on the beaches of Salerno, September 12, 1943. Hitler sent as many troops as he could to stop them. These fought with every kind of booby trap and gunfire.

The campaign up the peninsula was slow and costly, but by October the Allies took Naples. Then came another landing at Anzio.

After months of bloody fighting the Allied forces finally came within sight of Rome, the city of Caesar and a host of emperors and popes. They occupied the city on June 4, 1944. It was the first Axis capital to surrender to the Allies.

Now the Allied troops rolled on through the city and across the Tiber. They moved steadily northward through Tuscany to the Gothic Line, where the Germans had established their last line of resistance.

Patrol of Canadian and Indian soldiers on the lookout for enemy snipers in captured Rome

This was indeed a time of crisis. Many things were happening at once. The victory in Italy came when the Allies were poised for a strike at Western Europe. The Russians were battering the Germans in the East. And in the Pacific the long tentacles of the Japanese octopus were being chopped off one by one.

THE INVASION OF EUROPE

"No power on earth," boasted Hitler, "can drive us out!"

He was talking about what he called Fortress Europe, the great conquered continent which he had ringed with defenses. True, the Allies had already broken through the defenses in Italy. But along the shores of Normandy, facing England, was a maze of forts, tanks and artillery.

On the other side of the English Channel, the Allies were planning to undertake one of the biggest gambles of the war. They were going to attack the mighty Normandy defense system and try to invade Hitler's fortress. This was the famous Second Front. The First Front was in Russia.

The coming attack on France was called by a secret name — Operation Overlord. And the invasion day was called D-day.

May was the month chosen for this great venture. But the Allies had to wait for better weather. Storms arise suddenly over the English Channel. General Eisenhower, in command of the attack, had the grave responsibility of choosing exactly the right moment for it to begin.

First came a softening-up process. Huge waves of Allied bombers attacked the coastal defenses. They destroyed roads and bridges. Small units of commandos — fighters specially trained in sabotage and hand-to-hand combat — were dropped by plane to wreck the German radar stations. French resistance fighters were secretly supplied with weapons.

Meanwhile, war materials poured across the Atlantic from America. All England became a great military and supply base for the coming invasion. For months trucks and tanks rumbled along the roads. Planes roared overhead. From artillery ranges came the boom of practice shooting.

Then it came — June 6, 1944 — D-day!

At 2 o'clock in the morning British and American paratroopers dropped softly into Normandy. At 3 o'clock the heavy aerial bombardment began. At sunrise the big guns of the warships boomed. Artificial harbors made of concrete and old ships were towed into place to make calm waters for the invasion. These harbors were known by the code-names of Mulberry I and Mulberry II.

At last, from 4,000 transport ships that had crossed the Channel under cover of darkness, a huge army of men began to pour onto the Normandy beaches. The ships shuttled back and forth across the channel again and again. Warships and a great umbrella of planes protected them. It was the greatest display of military power in the history of the world.

Then suddenly the weather turned rough. Some of the amphibious tanks, which could be used both on water and on land, ran afoul of the German steel traps anchored along the beaches.

But the Germans were taken completely by surprise. They had made a series of blunders. Though they expected the invasion, they had thought that the weather was not right for it at that time. They had canceled a routine E-boat patrol that might have given them warning.

There was terrible fighting at the Normandy, or "Omaha" beach,

as the Americans called it. "Utah" beach, where other landings were made, was taken with less difficulty. And once the Allies had gained a foothold on the beaches they kept going forward. An Allied army of nearly a million men was landed in France.

Later, from the south of France, Allied armies began to push northward. This operation was known by the name of Anvil Dragoon. The Germans were caught in a trap. It was the beginning of the end of Hitler's empire.

Masses of men and equipment being landed on the coast of France from landing craft offshore

THE GENERAL SAYS "NUTS!"

By early December, 1944, six American armies together with the British were ready for an all-out attack on Hitler's Siegfried Line. The Germans, watching closely, decided to make one last desperate attempt to drive them back into the sea, just as they had done at Dunkirk.

The German commander, Marshal von Rundstedt, suddenly attacked in the Ardennes region of Belgium. He smashed ahead with one of the strongest tank forces in history. Soon his troops opened a tremendous hole, or bulge, in the Allied lines. This battle was called the Battle of the Bulge.

The Allies fought hard. They had no help from the air. The weather was so foggy that their planes could not get off the ground. One American unit was cut completely off at a small place called Bastogne in the middle of the Bulge. It looked like a bad Christmas for the British and the Americans.

At his headquarters the American General Anthony C. McAuliffe sat silent, wondering what to do next. An aide came in with a message from the Germans.

"What do they want?" asked the General.

"They demand our immediate surrender, sir!" said the officer. "And they want your reply at once."

"Tell them NUTS!" said the General.

That word became forever famous as an American symbol of defiance.

Then, as if by a miracle, the skies cleared. More than 5,000 Allied

The First Ski Patrol goes into action on the Ninth Army front in Germany during the winter 1944-45

warplanes swept into the air to pounce down on the advancing German tanks and bring them to a halt.

Meanwhile the American Generals Eisenhower, Bradley, and Patton, and the English General Montgomery sent reserves to Belgium to squeeze both sides of the Bulge. The bewildered Germans were forced back to their original positions.

This was the last German drive of the war. Prime Minister Churchill called the Battle of the Bulge the greatest American battle of the war.

At long last came the invasion into Germany.

General Patton's tanks went so fast that they ran out of gas. By good luck the Americans found a bridge at Remagen across the Rhine. The Germans, by a great blunder, had not blown up that precious bridge. American tanks sped across it.

Hitler had boasted that his Nazi Reich would last for a thousand years. But here it was cut in half and facing its end.

On May 8, 1945, Germany surrendered.

Two South African engineers display a Nazi flag they unearthed under a bombed hotel in Cassino, Italy

VICTORY ON THE SEAS

While these furious land battles were being fought, a battle just as important was being waged on and under the sea. The Nazis had renewed their U-boat campaign with even greater violence. But the Allies were winning this battle of the oceans.

For many months men in American and British naval laboratories had been working at top speed to perfect submarine-detecting devices. Now American and British aircraft of all types patrolled the blue oceans. These aircraft were equipped with radar sets specially built for detecting submarines. Regularly they kept watch over 80,000 miles of seaways, protecting as many as 3,000 ships at once.

Destroyers were equipped with a kind of underwater radar, called sonar, for locating submarines. Ships and aircraft worked together. If one detected submarines nearby, the other could be called in to help destroy them.

The tide of the sea battle turned against the Germans at the most critical stage of the war. For all the skill of the German submarine crews the power of the U-boat was shattered overnight. Radar changed everything. It robbed the Germans of their chief asset — invisibility in night attack.

By the end of 1943 and the beginning of 1944 the Germans were losing submarines at the rate of one a day. Altogether they had some 720 U-boats at sea. 640 of them were sunk. Out of 40,000 men who served in German U-boats, 30,000 lost their lives.

The Allies also defeated the Germans on the surface of the seas. On

December 26, 1943, for example, a British squadron fell upon the German battleship *Scharnhorst*. The battleship was trying to destroy a convoy on the way to Russia with supplies. The British squadron sent her to the bottom.

The mastery of the seas, which the Axis had seized in 1941, was now fully regained by the Allies.

Two depth bombs explode at the same time as a U. S. Navy *P.C.* boat fights a German submarine

66

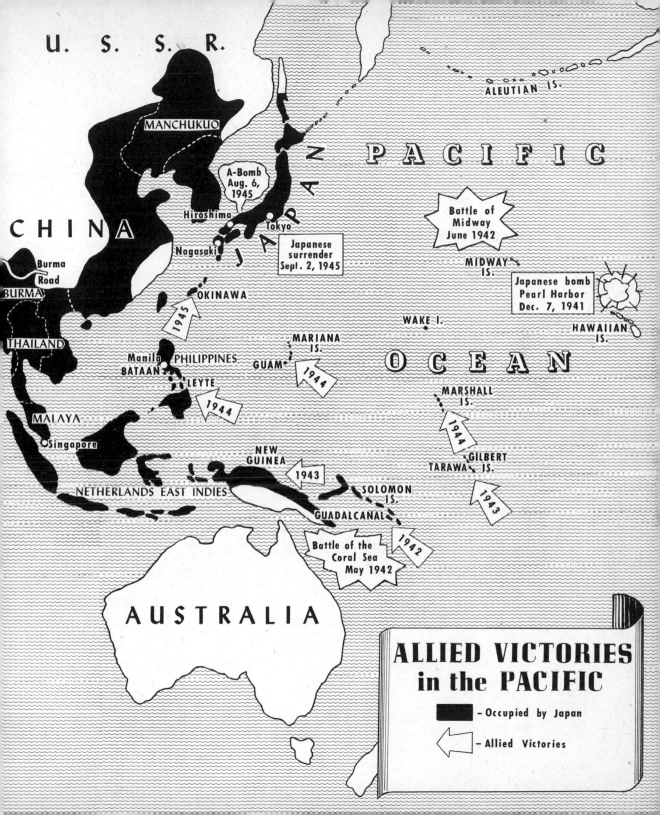

U. S. S. R.

MANCHUKUO

CHINA

PACIFIC

ALEUTIAN IS.

A-Bomb
Aug. 6,
1945

Hiroshima

Tokyo

JAPAN

Battle of
Midway
June 1942

Nagasaki

Japanese
surrender
Sept. 2, 1945

MIDWAY
IS.

Japanese bomb
Pearl Harbor
Dec. 7, 1941

Burma
Road

OKINAWA

1945

WAKE I.

OCEAN

HAWAIIAN
IS.

BURMA

THAILAND

MARIANA
IS.

Manila PHILIPPINES
BATAAN

GUAM

1944

MARSHALL
IS.

1944

LEYTE

1944

MALAYA

Singapore

NEW
GUINEA

1943

GILBERT
IS.

TARAWA

1943

NETHERLANDS EAST INDIES

SOLOMON
IS.

GUADALCANAL

1942

Battle of the
Coral Sea
May 1942

AUSTRALIA

**ALLIED VICTORIES
in the PACIFIC**

- Occupied by Japan

- Allied Victories

VICTORY IN THE PACIFIC

The Japanese made rapid conquests after their attack on Pearl Harbor. Before long the rubber, tin, oil, quinine, and other products of the East Indies were in their hands. Their conquered empire contained one-quarter of the earth's surface!

Then the American Navy began to fight back. Twice, in the middle of 1942, it thrashed the Japanese fleet soundly. These two American victories put an end to Japanese expansion.

The first battle, the Battle of the Coral Sea, took place in early May. It lasted six days. The Japanese and American surface fleets were too far apart even to see each other! Airplanes did the fighting. The defeated Japanese naval expedition abandoned its plan of attacking southern New Guinea.

The next month, on June 4, a Japanese squadron was discovered headed for Midway Island. Again American naval aircraft went into action. They mauled the Japanese squadron so badly that it retreated.

Now the American Navy was on the offensive. It was the attacker instead of the attacked. A strong American offensive took place on August 7, 1942, when United States Marines landed on Guadalcanal in the Solomon Islands.

The American plan for regaining a foothold in the Pacific was simple, but it was deadly. It consisted of a series of island "hops." From bases in the Solomon Islands American task forces would recapture one after another of the tiny islands seized by Japan. Each victory would bring them a step closer to Japan herself.

U. S. Marines slogging through tropical jungles,
moving up to attack the Japanese on Guadalcanal

U. S. Army Engineers carry a section of pipe through the Burmese jungle

First the Americans recaptured New Guinea. Then came Tarawa in the Gilbert Islands. Next were the Marshall Islands. Then there were the Marianas. As soon as one island was invaded the Americans were off to the next one.

By October of 1944, the Americans were ready to risk the daring leap to the Philippines. A huge Japanese naval force tried to halt the landings on Leyte over the period October 23-27, 1944. It lost two

Giant seagoing "freight cars" unload war cargoes on Leyte Island

U. S. Marines advance in the Solomon Islands, ever watchful for enemy snipers

A Coast Guard Combat Photographer snapped this war dog and his master seeking shelter in a fox-hole on Leyte Beach

battleships, four carriers, six heavy cruisers, three light cruisers, and about nine destroyers. It was a great American victory.

General MacArthur returned to the Philippines, just as he had promised.

Meanwhile, on the mainland of Southeast Asia, small bands of independent fighters, called guerilla fighters, carried on war deep behind the Japanese lines. They were under the command of the American General "Vinegar Joe" Stilwell and the British Brigadier General Wingate.

Slowly but surely the Allies built up their strength. They forced the Japanese out of Malaya, Thailand, Burma, and China.

With the capture of the island of Okinawa, the Americans advanced to within only 350 miles of the southern tip of the Japanese mainland. U. S. airmen rained tons of bombs down on the tinder-box cities of Japan.

A STORY OF COURAGE

Much of the success of the Allied campaign in the Pacific was due to the bravery and courage of the individual soldiers. Many times the British and Americans were cut off from guns, ammunition, and food. They were hungry a good part of the time. In the steaming jungles of the islands they dripped with sweat. Hordes of insects attacked them. They itched and burned with mosquito bites. Their feet were sore and swollen from the long marches and the jungle damp.

Then add to these hardships the nature of the enemy they had to fight. To a Japanese, his own personal welfare is not important. All that matters to him is the honor of his family. His family includes not only his mother and father, brothers and sisters, but the whole Japanese people, with the Emperor as the supreme "father."

The Japanese believe that it is better to commit suicide than to disgrace the "family." Because it would disgrace the family, they will not accept dishonor or defeat if they can help it. Every Japanese soldier is told that if he is about to be overcome by the enemy, or if he is captured, the only honorable thing to do is to kill himself.

While most armies would surrender to the enemy rather than sacrifice lives needlessly, the Japanese would not. The Allies in the Pacific found it almost impossible to make the Japanese surrender. They took very few prisoners. It was a fight to the death all the way.

Against these terrible odds the British and the Americans fought with a courage that the Axis had thought impossible in what they called the "soft" democracies.

U. S. Marines slosh their way through mud to the jungle front lines

BOMBS ON GERMANY

"Not a single Allied plane will appear over Berlin. If it does, you can call me 'Meyer'!"

That's what Hermann Goering said. He was the number two Nazi, head of the German Air Force.

A lot of Germans were to call him Meyer before long. They were very bitter about it.

The Germans were the first to start the bombing of cities in World War I. In the early part of World War II their planes devastated such great cities as Warsaw, Rotterdam, and London. Then the Allies struck back.

The first great Allied air attack was on Cologne, a city in the middle of the Rhineland. In the short space of 90 minutes more than a thousand planes showered the city with 2,000 tons of bombs.

In the weeks that followed the Germans were allowed no rest. During the day, American *Flying Fortresses* ranged all over the country. With the accurate Norden bomb-sight they hit their targets right on the nose.

At night came the giant British *Lancasters*. Each carried eight tons of "block-busters" — bombs so powerful that one of them could destroy an entire city block.

In between the *Fortresses* and the *Lancasters* came lighter British planes called *Mosquitoes*. Their buzzing was enough to keep the Germans awake and fearful through the night.

By 1943 the Allies had developed a new system of shuttle bombing.

American tank hit by mortar shell in devastated Cologne. In the background is the famous *Dom*, one of the most beautiful churches in the World. It was damaged but not destroyed by Allied airmen

Planes would fly over Germany, drop their clusters of bombs, and then head for North Africa. After resting a few days the pilots would return to England by way of Germany, dropping another load of bombs.

One after another the great cities of Germany were reduced to rubble. Hamburg was almost totally destroyed, and other cities were badly damaged. By 1945 Berlin was a shattered ghost-city.

It was a sad and terrible business. This was "total" war, invented by the Germans themselves. Civilians as well as soldiers were killed. Factories were destroyed. Homes were smashed.

The Germans were learning the hard way — what you do unto others can be done to you.

A French and a British soldier flee from a machine-gunning plane

British troops wire a tree felled across a canal to hold up the enemy

Hitler tried to strike back as best he could. His scientists were working on secret weapons which they believed would win the war for Germany. One of these was a flying, or "robot" bomb, called the V-1, or Vengeance Weapon No. 1. It was actually a small pilotless plane which carried a ton of explosives in its nose. Thousands of these flying bombs were launched from the Continent. They came screaming down on London.

Then the Germans began using the V-2, or flying rocket bomb. Much larger than the V-1, the V-2 could travel at 2,250 miles an hour. It was silent and gave no warning. It rose 60 miles into the stratosphere and then came down at terrific speed. It buried itself deeply into the ground before it exploded.

But these weapons came much too late. Germany was being pounded to pieces by round-the-clock bombings. She could not last much longer.

79

DEATH OF THREE LEADERS

On April 12, 1945, President Franklin D. Roosevelt died at Warm Springs, Georgia, three months after he had begun his fourth term as President. In his last speech, written to be delivered before Congress, his closing words were,

"Let us move forward with strong and active faith."

Roosevelt's death was a sad blow to Americans. Many men, women, and children broke down and cried when they heard the news.

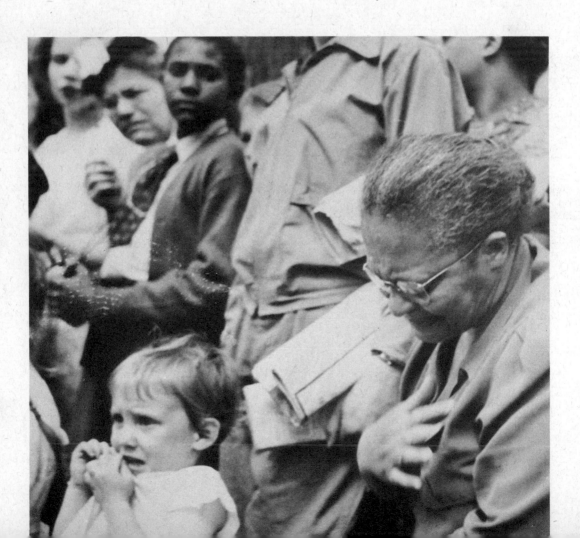

Three weeks later death came to the man who had wanted to be Caesar. Benito Mussolini's final boast, while Allied armies poured over Northern Italy, was that he would outdo Hitler in defeat.

"Between the two of us," he said, "the one who dies the more beautiful death will be a greater man in the eyes of history."

There was nothing beautiful about Mussolini's death. He tried to flee Italy in disguise, but he was captured by anti-Fascists.

"Let me save my life," he begged, "and I will give you an empire!"

His captors shot him. They strung up his bullet-ridden corpse by the heels outside a Milan filling station. Angry Italian citizens kicked and spat upon the body of the man who had brought them untold trouble and misery.

Two days later the German dictator, too, was dead.

Hitler was in an underground bunker, or shelter, below the streets of Berlin. Above him was a trembling, shattered city, a flaming ruin. Raving mad, he rushed from room to room. He ordered troops which did not exist into the path of the oncoming Russians.

"The German people are not worthy of me!" he shouted in agony.

Even at the last moment the mad dictator felt that he would be saved by some miracle. When the truth was forced on him he killed his wife of a few hours, Eva Braun. Then he put a bullet into his own mouth. The bodies were burned with gasoline in the yard.

Thus ended the life of one of the most vicious tyrants of all time. It took the combined might of three great World Powers to bring Hitler and his lunatic Nazis to the ground.

←

Some faces in the crowd as President Roosevelt's casket is carried through the gates of the White House

THE A-BOMB

Japan's navy and air force had been almost destroyed by August, 1945. But, by the *samurai,* or military code, the Japanese were honor bound to fight to the end. They turned the few planes they had left into flying bombs. Young Japanese pilots, after drinking a farewell toast, were strapped into their explosive-filled aircraft. Like human bombs, they aimed their planes at American warships and died in the explosions.

What could be done to bring an enemy like this to its knees? It was clear that the Allies would have to invade the home islands of Japan. A million Americans would probably be killed or wounded in this last great battle of the war.

But there was another solution to the problem.

The idea of nuclear fission, or splitting the atom, had long been known to physicists. If the power of the atom could be controlled, scientists could make a bomb of enormous power. Since the beginning of World War II both the Allies and the Axis had been racing to produce the first atomic bomb. There was real danger that the Germans would win the race.

Early in the war, Albert Einstein, the great German-born scientist who was now an American citizen, told President Roosevelt that such a bomb could be made. The President immediately set aside two billion dollars for research to produce the bomb. Many scientists worked on the project. There were the Italian Enrico Fermi, Lise Meitner — a German scientist who had escaped Nazi Germany — the Danish Nils

Bohr, the American J. Robert Oppenheimer, and many others. The bomb these scientists produced was a fearsome weapon.

Harry S. Truman, who became President after Roosevelt died, had a hard decision to make. Should he use this terrible weapon or not? He decided that it was the quickest way to end the war. He gave Japan fair warning, but she refused to surrender.

For months a vast American air armada had softened up the islands of Japan. Early in the morning of August 6, 1945, a giant Superfortress named *Enola Gay* took off for Japan. In her bomb bay was the A-bomb — a weapon that had in it the basic power of the universe. The city of Hiroshima, with a population of 344,000, had been selected as the target. In Hiroshima was located a small but important Japanese army base.

That one bomb had more power than 20,000 tons of TNT. It had 2,000 times the blast power of the largest bomb ever used until this time. It blew almost all of Hiroshima off the face of the earth. Houses collapsed like toys. Sheets of flame whipped through the city. Tens of thousands of panic-stricken people fled. Some had their eyebrows burned off. Others had skin hanging from their arms and faces. Terrorized birds flew off in every direction. The hills around the city swayed. There was an electric smell in the air. In seconds some 150,000 people were killed or wounded.

Hiroshima was covered with a huge rolling cloud of smoke and dust. First the heavens turned black. Then a giant mushroom cloud floated into the air. Gradually its deadly shape changed into a flower-like form.

This was a residential street in Hiroshima

Three days later an even more powerful A-bomb was dropped on Nagasaki, a city of 250,000 people.

After a week of silence the men who had planned the attack on Pearl Harbor saw that they had made a great mistake. Human courage could not compete with the atom gone crazy.

On September 2, 1945, the battleship *Missouri* lay at anchor in Tokyo Bay. Aboard her were the commanders of the Allied forces awaiting the arrival of the beaten Japanese.

Then a little launch appeared alongside the huge ship. The Japanese peace delegates stepped from it and came aboard the battleship. Silently they filed to a table set on the foredeck.

In a clear, firm voice General MacArthur read the terms of surrender. Everyone present was thinking of Pearl Harbor. General MacArthur finished reading and said,

"I now invite the representatives of Japan to sign the instrument of surrender at the places indicated."

Without a word the Japanese envoys wrote down their names.

"These proceedings are closed," said General MacArthur.

The war in the Pacific was over. It had lasted only three months longer than the war in Europe.

Japanese Foreign Minister Shigemitsu signs the surrender document that ended World War II. General MacArthur (left) and Lt. General Sutherland stand watching

THE PROBLEMS OF PEACE

World War II was the most expensive war in history. More than a trillion dollars were spent for war materials and armaments. But how can we measure the cost of broken lives, destroyed homes, the misery and poverty caused by war?

Germany lost 3,250,000 men in battle, Japan 1,500,000, and Italy 200,000. Among the Allies, Russia led with a loss of 3,000,000 killed in battle, the British Empire 400,000, the United States 325,000, and France 200,000.

The war was even more disastrous for civilians. 12,000,000 lost their lives. 35,000,000 were wounded. Not only bombs but starvation and disease took their dreadful toll.

When Italy, Germany, and finally Japan surrendered, the Allies entered the defeated Axis countries. Germany was split into four zones — British, American, French, and Russian. Those nations which had been occupied by the Axis were cleared of enemy troops.

For the first time in her history Japan learned what it meant to be occupied by a foreign people! Her Emperor was allowed to keep his throne because he was the only person who could persuade the Japanese people to submit peacefully to their conquerors. The military crowd was wiped out. Under General MacArthur, head of the occupation forces, the Japanese began to learn the ways of democracy.

When the Axis prison camps were opened, the world learned in full measure the horrors of Axis rule. The Allies did not let these war crimes against humanity go unpunished. The Nazis responsible for

86

Japanese children come on the run when American Occupation troops hand out chewing gum and candy

the death of millions of people in gas ovens were put on trial in Nuremberg. Nineteen were found guilty and either executed or sentenced to long prison terms. Hermann Goering killed himself with poison a few minutes before he was to be hanged.

The terrible price which Europe had paid for submission to Hitler was now clear. It is difficult to understand how he gained such power over intelligent people. Most difficult to understand is why the Germans themselves did not stop him in the beginning. He made it quite clear, in his speeches and in his book, *Mein Kampf,* what he was up to. Some did try to stop him, of course, and they paid terrible penalties. But most went along with him, even though he carried out his horrible cruelties right under their eyes. For this they must remain responsible before the world and before history.

PLANNING A PEACEFUL WORLD

After World War II, the United States and the Soviet Union became the two greatest powers on earth. The great problem now was, how could these two countries live in peace?

Before the war ended, the diplomats of the Big Three — the United States, Great Britain, and Soviet Russia — had made temporary plans to insure a peaceful world. At the Yalta Conference, over the period February 4-11, 1945, they had agreed that the liberated, or freed, peoples of Europe should be allowed to form democratic governments of their own choice. But Russia did not live up to her part of the agreement. Before long she established "satellite" states in Eastern Europe.

The word "satellite" means a small star which revolves around a larger one. The satellite states were meant to revolve around Russia and do as she told them. Russia seized control of such countries as Hungary and Czechoslovakia in spite of her promises at Yalta.

At the last wartime conference, held at Potsdam, Germany, from July 17 to August 2, 1945, the Allies fixed the peace terms for defeated Germany. Then the wartime friendship between the Big Three evaporated. Russia turned her back on her allies and tried to draw other countries to her side. Believing she was not safe in a democratic world, she plunged ahead with a plan to draw more and more countries into the Communist dictatorship.

The United States and Great Britain refused to recognize her right to do this.

THE UNITED NATIONS

After World War I, the world tried to prevent more wars by forming a League of Nations where countries could settle their disagreements peacefully. But the League disappointed many people. Its weakness was that it was an organization of governments, not peoples.

The Charter of the United Nations, formed after World War II for the same purpose as the League, starts out with the words, "We the peoples ..."

The Charter of the United Nations was signed at San Francisco on June 26, 1945, by the delegates of 50 countries.

The United Nations is a kind of town meeting of the world, where delegates of the member nations can meet and discuss their problems. When nations quarrel it is better to talk things over than to go to war.

Perhaps most important of all, the United Nations tries to prevent the things that have led to war in the past. It has even made peace between nations that had already started to fight.

Various branches of the United Nations work hard in other ways to prevent the things that lead to war. The Economic and Social Council helps poor people all over the world, for we know that poverty can help to breed war.

The World Health Organization, WHO, advises member countries on public health and the control of disease. It makes war on plagues such as malaria, tuberculosis, and on less common diseases such as leprosy, typhus, polio, and diphtheria, and in emergencies sends planes with doctors and drugs from one country to the other.

Headquarters for the United Nations in New York. At the left is the United Nations Secretariat building. The domed building to the right is the General Assembly Hall, backed by the New York skyline

The International Labor Organization, ILO, helps workers throughout the world, not only with their own problems but also with worldwide labor problems. It teaches all workers to know and understand each other better.

The Educational, Scientific, and Cultural Organization, UNESCO, gives useful information to all countries.

One of the weaknesses of the United Nations is the rule called the veto clause. What this means is that any one of the big nations on the Security Council — the United States, Britain, Russia, France, or Nationalist China — can veto, or forbid, talking about any question which it does not want to discuss.

One of the most difficult problems of the United Nations has been that of disarmament, or reducing the armed forces of the world. A future World War is unthinkable. We have developed far too terrible weapons — the hydrogen bomb, and guided missiles which can span a continent. Any all-out war would result in the destruction of most of mankind.

But the nations must take the first step toward disarmament of their own free wills. They must list their armed forces with the United Nations and tell plainly and honestly how many there are at home and in foreign countries. The United Nations has been trying to have all the nations of the world permit a special committee to make a full inspection of their armaments.

The way of the United Nations has been neither easy nor happy. But the important thing is that the road to peace is still open.

Some people say that there has always been war and that there always will be. Let us not be too sure of that. Once men lived by the code of the duel. If a man thought he had been insulted, he would demand that the man who had insulted him fight it out in a duel. This old-fashioned idea died out as people began to have more respect for the law as a means of obtaining justice.

So it is with the nations in the world today. As their respect for law increases, the nations will turn to the United Nations instead of going to war.

We live in an atomic age. Not many of us could survive an atomic war. We will live in one world, abiding by laws created for the good of all people, or we will not live at all.

We must win a victory over war itself. That is the hope of the civilized world.

WORLD WAR II WORDS

A-BOMB: The atomic bomb.

ALLIES: Great Britain, France, United States, Russia, China, and many smaller countries.

ATLANTIC WALL: German control of the ports of Western Europe.

AXIS or AXIS POWERS: Germany, Italy, and Japan.

BANZAI ATTACK: Reckless bayonet charge by Japanese soldiers with yells of "Banzai!" This means, "10,000 years, forever!"

BLITZKRIEG, or *BLITZ*: Lightning war: swift-moving air and ground attacks by German armies.

BLOCKBUSTERS: Big British bombs.

BURMA ROAD: Supply route to China.

CASE BARBAROSSA: Hitler's plan for crushing Russia.

COLLABORATORS: Traitors who helped the Axis inside conquered countries.

DER FUEHRER: The leader; used by the Germans in referring to the Nazi leader, Adolf Hitler.

FASCIST: Badge of authority; the name of the party founded in Italy by Mussolini.

F.F.I.: French forces of the Interior; French fighters for freedom from the Nazis.

FLAT-TOPS: Aircraft carriers.

FLYING FORTRESS: Heavy American bombing plane.

GOTHIC LINE: Final German battle line in North Italy.

GREATER EAST-ASIA CO-PROSPERITY SPHERE: Japanese name for their conquered empire in early years of World War II.

HURRICANE: British fighter plane.

IL DUCE: The leader; the Italian Fascists' name for their leader, Mussolini.

ISLAND HOPPING: The U. S. plan to hop, skip, and jump from one island to another to the heart of Japan.

KAMIKAZES: Japanese suicide pilots.

LANCASTER: Heavy British bombing plane.

LEND-LEASE ACT: U. S. help for Britain, March 11, 1941.

LUFTWAFFE: The German Air Force.

MAGINOT LINE: French underground line of forts along the Franco-German border.

MAQUIS: French resistance fighters.

MESSERSCHMITT: German fighter plane.

MULBERRY HARBORS: Artificial harbors made especially for the Normandy invasion.

MURMANSK RUN: North Atlantic sea lane for help to Russia.

NAZIS: Followers of Hitler.

O.P.A.: Office of Price Administration; U. S. agency to fix wages and prices, January, 1942.

OPERATION OVERLORD: Code name for the Allied invasion of Normandy.

OPERATION SEA LION: Code name for Hitler's plan to invade England, which was never carried out.

OPERATION TORCH: Code name for the invasion of North Africa.

PEARL HARBOR: U. S. naval base in Hawaii; attacked by the Japanese on December 7, 1941.

RADAR: The electronic "eye" which sees through fog and darkness.

R.A.F.: Royal Air Force of Great Britain.

RED DEVILS: 1st British Airborne Division.

SECOND FRONT: The Allied line against Germany in Western Europe.

SIEGFRIED LINE: German Defense line facing France.

SITZKRIEG: "Sit-down" or "phony" war, on the Western Front, 1939 to early 1940.

SPITFIRE: British Fighter plane.

STORMOVIK: Russian ground-strafing plane.

THIRD REICH: Hitler's Nazi state.

TOKYO ROSE: Japanese girl who sent out radio appeals in English for the Allied troops to surrender.

U-BOATS: Submarines.

V-1: Vengeance weapon; Nazi flying bomb.

PICTURE CREDITS

Jacket, F.P.G.

Half-title page, United Press

Title page, United Press

Contents page, United Press

Page 6, United Press

Page 9, upper left, F.P.G.; upper right, Wide World; lower right, United Press

Page 11, F.P.G.

Page 13, F.P.G.

Page 15, United Press

Page 17, United Press

Page 19, F.P.G.

Page 20, United Press

Page 23, F.P.G.

Page 25, Youssuf Karsh

Page 26, United Press

Page 27, F.P.G.

Page 31, F.P.G.

Page 32, United Press

Page 33, United Press

Page 34, F.P.G.

Page 35, F.P.G.

Page 39, Sovfoto

Page 41, Sovfoto

Page 43, F.P.G.

Page 44, United Press

Page 47, United Press

Page 49, United Press

Page 50, United Press

Page 53, F.P.G.

Pages 60-61, upper left, United Press

Page 61, lower right, F.P.G.

Page 63, F.P.G.

Page 64, F.P.G.

Page 66, F.P.G.

Page 69, United Press

Page 70, F.P.G.

Page 71, F.P.G.

Page 72, United Press

Page 73, Official Coast Guard, F.P.G.

Page 75, United Press

Page 77, F.P.G.

Page 78, F.P.G.

Page 79, F.P.G.

Page 80, United Press

Page 84, United Press

Page 85, Wide World

Page 87, United Press

Page 90, United Press

INDEX

INDEX